& CHRISSIE

The Greatest Rivalry in the History of Sports

Phil Bildner   illustrated by Brett Helquist

CANDLEWICK PRESS

Hey, guys—
yeah, I'm talking to you.
You see those two names on the cover?
Martina and Chrissie?
That's Martina Navratilova and Chris Evert.

You know who they are, right? No?
NO?!

Wow, okay.

Well, these two women
formed the greatest rivalry in the history of sports.
No, not the history of women's sports—
the history of **ALL** sports.

Yeah, you **NEED** to know about Martina and Chrissie.

MARTINA

First, let me tell you about Chrissie:
She started taking lessons when she was five.
By eighth grade, she was ranked number one
in the **WHOLE** country.

Chrissie was this All-American girl.
Patience and poise and precision.
Calm and collected and completely in control.
Her ground strokes were perfect, perfect.
From the baseline, she was automatic, automatic.
And that two-handed backhand of hers—oh, man!
Everyone copied the way she hit it.
EVERYONE!

In 1971, she played in her first-ever Grand Slam tournament,
the U.S. Open.

"Little Chrissie Evert" against Mary Ann Eisel, the fourth-ranked woman
in the country, on center court at Forest Hills.

She lost the first set, fell behind in the second,
and the TV announcers wrote her off.

But then the high-school girl from Florida fought off six match points—
SIX!
She won the match. Won. The. Match.

Nah, she didn't win the tournament.
She won something better: the hearts of the fans.

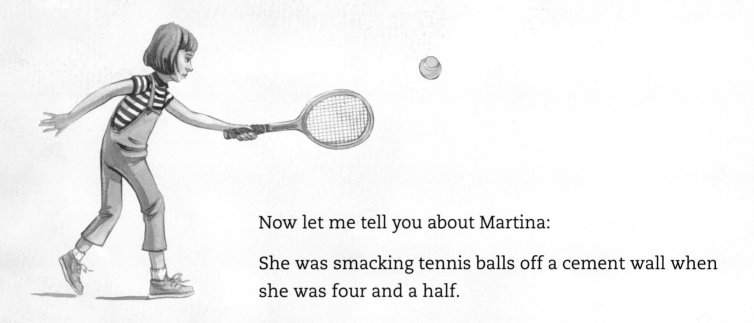

Now let me tell you about Martina:

She was smacking tennis balls off a cement wall when she was four and a half.

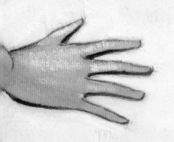

At fifteen, she was the national champ.
FIFTEEN!

But Martina was from Czechoslovakia,
a Communist country.

In Communist countries, you weren't free.
Not like America, not at all.

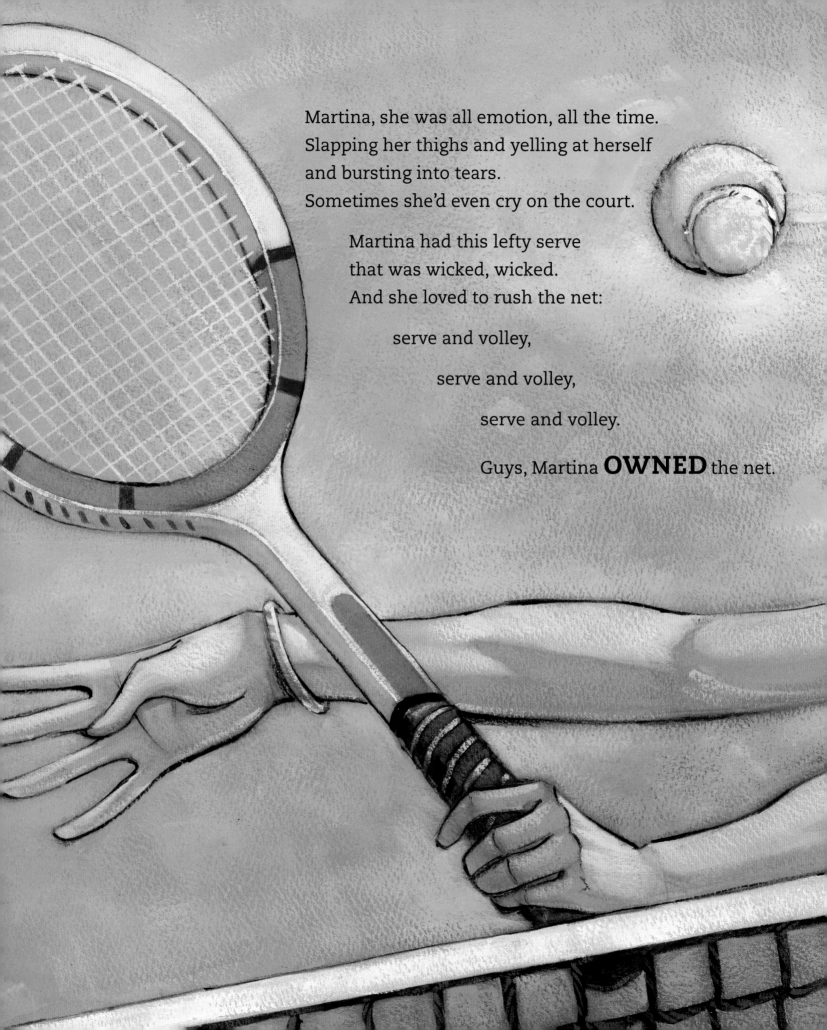

Martina, she was all emotion, all the time.
Slapping her thighs and yelling at herself
and bursting into tears.
Sometimes she'd even cry on the court.

Martina had this lefty serve
that was wicked, wicked.
And she loved to rush the net:

serve and volley,

serve and volley,

serve and volley.

Guys, Martina **OWNED** the net.

But at the time,
that's not how women were *supposed* to play tennis.
Not in the United States.
Women were expected to act a certain way,
behave a certain way.

Martina said, **"NO."**
She was going to play *her* brand of tennis
whether you liked it or not.

Keep in mind, this was during the Cold War.
You do know what the Cold War was, right? No?

The Cold War was when the two greatest powers on the
planet—the United States, a free country,
and the Soviet Union, a Communist country—
were locked in a standoff.

For decades, the two nations distrusted each other,
despised each other, wanted to destroy each other.
For decades, the nations of the world picked sides.

Martina was from the other side.

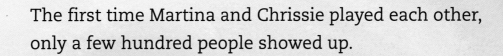

The first time Martina and Chrissie played each other,
only a few hundred people showed up.

Martina was out of shape.
REALLY out of shape.
And Chrissie won.
Easily.

In fact, those first few years they played,
Chrissie flat-out dominated.
Then again, Chrissie dominated everyone.

For five years in a row, she was the number one player
on the planet.
On. The. Planet.

Most rivals don't like each other.
Some rivals **HATE** each other.

And because of the Cold War,
Martina and Chrissie were supposed to distrust and
despise and want to destroy each other, too.

But Martina and Chrissie,
they were friends,
good friends.

Before matches, they hung out, watched television,
ate meals, and even practiced together.

Martina and Chrissie, they weren't the type of women
who did what they were *supposed* to do.

After a while, Martina got tired of all that losing.
Even to her friend.

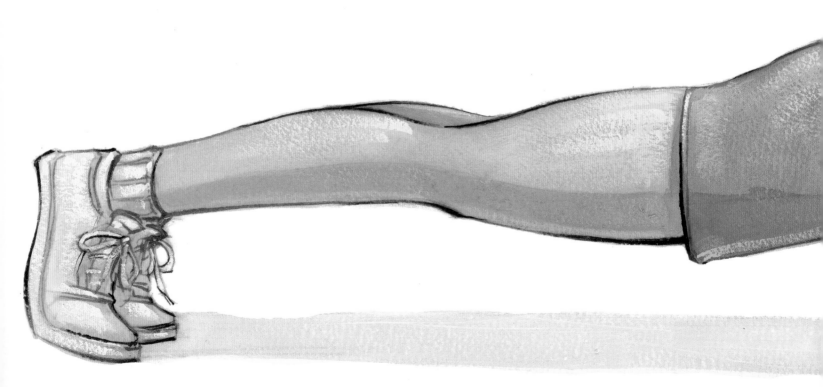

So she did something about it.
She got in shape.
She grew up.

Then came the Wimbledon where Martina and Chrissie played in the finals.

At first, Chrissie was rolling like always.

On this one point, Martina was at the net for an easy overhead smash,

but then a gust of wind blew and Martina
WHIFFED!

On another point, Martina was at the net and Chrissie blasted a shot that—

BAM!

nailed Martina right in the head.
Well, guys, that shot woke Martina up.

She fought off three break points. **THREE!**

Won the game.

Won the set.

Won the match.

Martina, Wimbledon champion, her first Grand Slam title.

Over the next few years . . .

Chrissie won,

Martina won,

Martina won,

Chrissie won.

The two best players in the world doing battle, back and forth, back and forth.

Each Sunday that Martina and Chrissie played, everyone tuned in to watch.

But then something changed between Martina and Chrissie.

Martina got a new coach with a new approach. And this new coach, she didn't allow her players to be friends with their rivals. She wanted them to hate their opponents. Like enemies.

For a few years, Martina and Chrissie barely spoke.

On the courts, Martina went on a rampage.
She beat Chrissie thirteen straight times.
THIRTEEN!
All in the finals of tournaments!

Second set, Martina.

Third set, oh, man!
Chrissie was one game
from the match,
ONE game from the title.

But then Chrissie rallied back.
On match point—
BOOM!

But Chrissie, she never gave up or gave in.
At the French Open, they met in the finals.
Martina seeded number one, Chrissie number two.
Neither having dropped a single set in the entire
tournament.

First set, Chrissie.

But Martina rallied,
took twelve of the
next thirteen points.

she smoked a monster backhand
down the line.
Game. Set. Match.
Chrissie was queen again.

But this time around, she shared her crown with Martina.
Her rival, her friend.

You see, for all those years,
Martina never gave up or gave in either.
And finally, she'd earned something more valuable than
any championship.

She won the hearts of the fans.

So who was better? Martina or Chrissie?

Martina and Chrissie played eighty times.
Martina won forty-three.

Sixty of those matches took place in tournament finals.
Martina won thirty-six.

Fourteen of those tournaments were Grand Slams.
Martina won ten.

So if you go by the numbers, it's pretty clear.
Advantage, Martina.
But guys, numbers **NEVER** tell the whole story.
And no rivalry is ever just about numbers.

Martina Navratilova and Chris Evert made each other
better players, and better people, too.

Because they played together, they became the best,
equal parts of the greatest rivalry in the history of sports.

MARTINA AND CHRISSIE THROUGH THE YEARS

1960s

Martina grew up in Řevnice, Czechoslovakia, a rural town outside Prague. At the time, the Communist party ruled Czechoslovakia and controlled almost every aspect of the lives of the citizens.

Chrissie was raised in Fort Lauderdale, Florida. Jimmy Evert, her father and a local tennis pro, spent countless hours with her, practicing on the clay courts.

1971

Chrissie burst onto the scene at the U.S. Open, her first Grand Slam tournament. In a stunning comeback on center court, she defeated Mary Ann Eisel, who was ranked fourth in the country, fighting off three match points. Chrissie then pulled off two more riveting, come-from-behind wins before losing to eventual champion Billie Jean King.

1973

On March 22, 1973, in the opening round of the Akron Tennis Open, Martina and Chrissie played each other for the first time. Chrissie defeated Martina, 7–6, 6–3.

1975

After losing to Chrissie in the semifinals of the 1975 U.S. Open, Martina defected to the United States. At the time, citizens of Communist countries—like Czechoslovakia—were not permitted to relocate to the United States or other countries. If they did, they did so illegally. Incredibly, Chrissie knew that Martina was about to make the risky and dangerous move even as they played their match.

Mid-1970s

For a brief period, Martina and Chrissie played a number of doubles tournaments together. They won two Grand Slam titles, the 1975 French Open and the 1976 Wimbledon championship.

Head-to-head, Chrissie won 21 of the first 25 matches she played against Martina. In more than half of those matches, she beat Martina in straight sets.

1978

Martina played in her first Wimbledon singles final. Martina's parents, who still lived in Communist Czechoslovakia, had promised Martina (before her defection) that if she ever made it to the finals of Wimbledon, they would drive to the border of West Germany so they could watch the match on German television. On the day of the match, Martina didn't know if her parents were even aware she was playing. They were. They watched. Just like they promised.

1981

Following a crushing and embarrassing 6–0, 6–0 loss to Chrissie, Martina completely changed her approach to tennis. She started working with basketball star Nancy Lieberman and tennis star Renée Richards. Lieberman helped Martina with her strength and conditioning. Richards helped Martina with her on-court strategies. Together, they became known as Team Navratilova. At the time, many ridiculed this new approach, but it marked a turning point in tennis and sports training. Soon, other athletes began following the Team Navratilova model.

Early 1980s

Martina dominated the world of women's tennis. From 1982 to 1985, she won 355 matches and lost only 10. During one stretch, she won 74 consecutive matches, the all-time record in women's tennis, and 6 straight Grand Slam titles.

1985

Martina and Chrissie's classic showdown in the finals of the 1985 French Open was one of the greatest matches in the tournament's history. In the nearly three-hour-long roller-coaster duel, Chrissie outlasted Martina 6–3, 6–7, 7–5. With the win,

Chrissie became the number one player in the world for the fifth and final time of her career.

1986

For the second year in a row, Martina and Chrissie faced off in an epic duel in the finals of the French Open. Once again, Chrissie was the victor, defeating her rival, 2–6, 6–3, 6–3. For Chrissie, it was a record seventh French Open title.

1989

Chrissie retired from tennis having won a total of 18 Grand Slam singles titles and at least one Grand Slam title for 13 consecutive years (1974–1986). She reached the semifinals or finals in her first 34 Grand Slam tournaments and in 52 of 56 overall.

1990

At the age of thirty-three, Martina won her ninth Wimbledon crown, breaking the record she shared with Helen Wills Moody.

1994

Martina retired from full-time singles competition. She had won a total of 167 tournaments and 1,438 matches. No player—male or female—has ever won more. She also won 344 doubles tournaments, more than any other player in history.

Life After Tennis

To this day, Martina and Chrissie remain as close as ever, supporting each other in their efforts and endeavors. After retiring, Chrissie founded the Chris Evert Charities, which helps fund programs for at-risk children and their families. Over the years, Martina has participated in numerous celebrity tennis fund-raising events for the foundation. Chrissie continues to support Martina in her role as a leading advocate for equality and gay rights, especially in the world of sports.

"Whenever something big happens in our lives, we're in touch immediately," said Chrissie in an interview with ESPN. "We've got each other's back."

They most certainly do.

SOURCES

Books

Flink, Steve. *The Greatest Tennis Matches of All Time*. Chicago: New Chapter Press, 2012.

Howard, Johnette. *The Rivals: Chris Evert vs. Martina Navratilova: Their Epic Duels and Extraordinary Friendship*. New York: Broadway, 2006.

Miller, Stuart. *The 100 Greatest Days in New York Sports*. Boston: Houghton Mifflin, 2006.

Ware, Susan. *Game, Set, Match: Billie Jean King and the Revolution in Women's Sports*. Chapel Hill: University of North Carolina Press, 2011.

Articles

Lazarus, Adam. "Top 100 Rivalries in Sports History." Bleacher Report. February 13, 2011. http://bleacherreport.com/articles/607334-top-100-rivalries-in-sports-history.

Levy, Glen. "Top 10 French Open Moments." Time.com. May 21, 2009. http://www.time.com/time/specials/packages/article/0,28804,1900153_1900155_1900157,00.html.

Schwartz, Larry. "Evert: Grit, Grace and Glamour." ESPN.com. http://espn.go.com/sportscentury/features/00014187.html.

———. "Martina Was Alone on Top." ESPN.com. http://espn.go.com/sportscentury/features/00016378.html.

Tignor, Steve. "Martina's Moment." Tennis.com. April 29, 2013. http://blogs.tennis.com/thewrap/2011/11/high-strung-the-lost-chapters-martinas-moment.html.

World Tennis Magazine. "The Fascinating Story Behind Martina Navratilova's Defection to the USA." October 18, 2010. http://www.worldtennismagazine.com/archives/3532.

Zaldivar, Gabe. "The 100 Best Rivalries in Sports." Bleacher Report. November 24, 2010. http://bleacherreport.com/articles/526637-100-best-rivalries.

Audiovisual

"Chris Evert vs. Martina Navratilova—1985 French Open final (Part 1 of 2)." YouTube video, 10:53. Posted on June 1, 2010. http://www.youtube.com/watch?v=w4DjYsAYCBM.

ESPN Films. "Unmatched," *30 for 30*. Directed and produced by Lisa Lax and Nancy Stern Winters. Co-produced by Hannah Storm. 2010. DVD, 51 min.

Websites

Chris Evert's website: http://chrisevert.net/.

"Chris Evert." International Tennis Hall of Fame website: http://www.tennisfame.com/hall-of-famers/inductees/chris-evert.

Martina Navratilova's website: http://www.martinanavratilova.com/.

"Martina Navratilova." International Tennis Hall of Fame website: http://www.tennisfame.com/hall-of-famers/inductees/martina-navratilova.

For Dennis, for listening to me read this over and over
and over in Port Ludlow, and for Eddie, my tennis buddy
P. B.

To Mary Jane
B. H.

First paperback edition 2019

Library of Congress Catalog Card Number 2017931502
ISBN 978-0-7636-7308-6 (hardcover)
ISBN 978-1-5362-0564-0 (paperback)

19 20 21 22 23 24 CCP 10 9 8 7 6 5 4 3 2 1

Printed in Shenzhen, Guangdong, China

This book was typeset in Caecilia.
The illustrations were done in acrylic and oil on paper.

Candlewick Press
99 Dover Street
Somerville, Massachusetts 02144

visit us at www.candlewick.com